Lines from an Ordinary Life
(LOL)

Lines from an Ordinary Life (LOL)

SALLY LANG

Copyright © 2025 Sally Lang

The moral right of the author has been asserted.

Apart from any fair dealing for the purposes of research or private study, or criticism or review, as permitted under the Copyright, Designs and Patents Act 1988, this publication may only be reproduced, stored or transmitted, in any form or by any means, with the prior permission in writing of the publishers, or in the case of reprographic reproduction in accordance with the terms of licences issued by the Copyright Licensing Agency. Enquiries concerning reproduction outside those terms should be sent to the publishers.

The manufacturer's authorised representative in the EU for product safety is Authorised Rep Compliance Ltd, 71 Lower Baggot Street, Dublin D02 P593 Ireland
(www.arccompliance.com)

This is a work of fiction. Names, characters, businesses, places, events and incidents are either the products of the author's imagination or used in a fictitious manner. Any resemblance to actual persons, living or dead, or actual events is purely coincidental.

Troubador Publishing Ltd
Unit E2 Airfield Business Park,
Harrison Road, Market Harborough,
Leicestershire. LE16 7UL
Tel: 0116 2792299
Email: books@troubador.co.uk
Web: www.troubador.co.uk

ISBN 978-1-83628-483-3

British Library Cataloguing in Publication Data.
A catalogue record for this book is available from the British Library.

Printed and bound in Great Britain by 4edge Limited
Typeset in 11pt Minion Pro by Troubador Publishing Ltd, Leicester, UK

For Alan, Jen and Alistair
with love

Lines from an Ordinary Life (LOL)

I don't claim for a second that these collected poems are a work of great literature. I am astonished at the works of other poets: their immense vocabularies and wordsmithing, their intellect and imagination. I do think, however, that there is a place out there for simpler, more down-to-earth poems that, hopefully, connect with people's experiences in today's complicated world.

I hope very much that you enjoy my scribblings.

Sally x

Contents

Poems to Make You Smile

A True Story	1
What Is This Thing…	2
A List of Impossible Things	3
True Story Number Two	5
Apparently…	7
The Bathroom Scales	9
What If…	11
Beer Mat Wisdom	12
Mushy Peas	13
Chippy Date	14
Hobbies, a History	16
Letter to My Thirteen-Year-Old Self	18
Lumbar Lament	20
Massage in a Northern Town	22
The Mind Reader	24
The Should Shouters	26
The Very Hungry Dieter	28

Poems About Motherhood

Maternal Roller Coaster	32
Little Brother	33
Do You Remember?	34
Lines to a Daughter…	36
Mother and Child	38
Nobody Told Me	40
Waiting to be a Granny	42
One Day	44

Poems About Life, Love and Grief

I Am Made From	48
My Mum…	49
Still…	51
March Morning, 1954	52
The Shared Peach	54
Today	55
The Shed	57
My Song	58
I'm Sorry	60
Weight of Grief	62
Anstey's Cove, 1933	64
Dark Days…	66
Have My Seat	67

Don't Assume You Know	68
Facts	70
I'm Fine	72
Last Night…	74
Most of the Time	76

Miscellaneous Poems

Enough	80
Autumn Lines	82
Canal Cormorant (Phalacrocorax Carbo)	84
Drizzle	86
Hidden Agenda	88
If I'm Honest…	90
Turning a Blind Eye	92
Shocked by My Own Lethargy	94
Autumn's Approach	96
Grandma	97
Someone Else's Tune	98
About the Author	101

Poems to Make You Smile

These poems were all written about mundane, quirky, unique and often amusing (I hope) happenings. There are events in everyone's ordinary lives, I think, that can make you smile, sometimes at the absurdities of life and, more often, I find, a realisation that I am, in fact, turning into my mother. I hope they tickle your funny bones.

A True Story

you gave me roses
for my birthday
twenty-one long-stemmed blooms
of the deepest red
and you said
if memory serves me right
on that sultry
romantic
summer's
night,
'do you know how much they cost?'

What Is This Thing...

'What is this thing called love?'
he asked, and I gasped.
'Wow! That's pretty profound
for a Wednesday morning
I guess,' I replied thoughtfully.
'It's that glow when you know that you've got each
 other's back,
it's the lack of aloneness,
but no, that's not quite right,
it's the butterflies at the sight of you after an absence,
even after all this time,
the wine you pour me at the end of the day,
the way you hold my hand when we cross the street,
the sweetness of your kiss
and so much more – but will that do for now?'
'No,' he said,
'I mean what is this thing called, love?'
'Oh, that's the new can opener, Trevor.'

A List of Impossible Things

A list of things I find impossible:
drinking a single glass of wine,
now – sadly,
lying in bed after 8am,
eating just one Jaffa cake,
drinking coffee
even though I love the smell,
getting out of a chair without grunting,
taking just the right number of
bags to the shop,
knowing the difference between
a plant and a weed,
these days
threading a needle without a magnifying glass,
passing a garage without commenting on
the price of fuel,
watching *Bargain Hunt* without saying
'we could do better than that',
listening to *The Archers* without
falling asleep,
wearing a pale-coloured top
without spilling food down it
within the first five minutes,
keeping white bras white,

painting the nails on my right hand,
accurately applying eyeliner,
throwing away clothes that I will never,
ever slim into,
wearing uncomfortable shoes
because they look good,
cleaning behind the radiators,
silently judging the contents
of other people's shopping trolleys,
tutting and grumbling when supermarkets
load up Christmas aisles in September,
using a silly voice when talking to dogs,
smiling when I'm hugged,
laughing
when I read the ridiculousness of this list
and realise that
I'm turning into my mother.

True Story Number Two

We went swimming – do you remember?
To the council pool after work
in the cool of the evening
and the chlorinated, echoing space
rang with squeals and peals of delight.
Red-eyed, wrinkled children
and stern-faced lifeguards
glaring hard at the dive-bombers
and slippery-tiled runners
and we stripped and stored our clothes
in metal lockers
donning swimsuits and flesh-pinching
coloured rubber bands to show,
when our colour was called,
that we had to leave the pool
or be hauled out, shamefaced,
and our friend couldn't fit
his prosthetic leg into the locker
and hopped to leave it with the
pimpled attendant
and we swam and laughed and dived
and when we pulled ourselves,
dripping,
from the churned water,

our friend hopped once more
to restore his plastic leg to its stump
and said,
'Can I have my leg back?'
and the attendant,
without a moment's hesitation,
asked,
'Is it yours?'

Apparently...

Apparently I should be standing on one leg
When I brush my teeth
In the belief
That it will stop me
Falling over when I'm ninety.

Apparently I should be moisturising
Every night with hyaluronic acid
So that when I fall and break my hip
At ninety
I won't have any wrinkles,
My face will be placid and smooth.

Apparently I should be eating
Kiwis at least four times a day
To keep dementia at bay
So that when I fall and break my hip
At ninety
Not only will I be wrinkle-free
But will gleefully recite the name of
The prime minister.

Apparently I should be doing
Regular down dogs on my mat
So that
When I fall and break my hip
At ninety
I will be wrinkle-free,
Know the name of the prime minister
And be able to stretch the unbroken femur
Round the back of my neck.

Apparently,
And it's just occurred to me,
I'm a bit sick of being told what to do.

The Bathroom Scales

I have a close relationship with the scales
on my bathroom floor,
they've been with me through fat and thin since 1974,
they can dictate my daily mood,
whether I laugh or frown,
by showing me in digits large if my weight is up or down.

bizarrely, if I've lost a pound after a week of being 'good',
it's easy to forgo those crisps and that leftover Christmas pud,
but heaven forbid, if my week's abstinence
is met with a half-pound gain,
I'm raiding the fridge, and the biscuit tin, crying, 'I'm never dieting again!'

I'm beginning to think they're a 'toxic' friend,
one I should really ignore,
they've tutted at me for far too long and dieting's such a bore.
so it's off to the dump, scales in tow, I'll chuck them in the skip with glee,
and I promise, no more weighing myself, let's end this tyranny!

from now I won't count calories, I'll rate healthiness instead,
and about how much I've lost or gained, nothing will be said,
so if you've ever heard yourself vow 'I mustn't eat that today',
join with me, free yourself and throw your scales away!

What If...

she said,
turning from the sink,
'Do you ever think
if we'd never met,
you didn't get that last bus home,
we'd never known each other
and our children had had different genes,
would that mean
you'd be washing up,
not me?'

Beer Mat Wisdom

I saw a beer mat in a bar
in Kuala Lumpur (don't ask)
and though its task may have been
to get me to buy gin
or something,
what I noticed instead
in letters of bright red
it said,
'I want a man to look at me
the way I look at food'
and I thought,
who knew that men like that existed?

Mushy Peas

you're the sausage to my mash
you're the fish with my mushy peas
you're the egg on my corned beef hash
you're the pickle with my cheese

you're the olive in my martini
the lime in my chilled margherita
you're the tonic in my gin
the chilli in my fajita

without you I'm a cake without icing
without you I'm a vinegar-less chip
without you I'm a flower with no perfume
I'm a pancake with no flip

without you my days are much duller
the sunshine never breaks through
and the rain is somehow wetter
whenever I'm without you

I'm not at my best flying solo
on my own doesn't feel quite so strong
so stay with me my second self
together is where we belong

Chippy Date

he was older than me
and that mattered
I was flattered
by his attention
not to mention
the looks
we exchanged
as we changed our books
in the library
and he asked me out
on a date
and I waited
while my beating heart
slowed
before I said,
'alright then.'

he said in his sophisticated way
that he'd meet me on Saturday
outside the chippy on the high street
we'd meet
at twelve noon
and he'd buy me chips

and soon I was waiting
in my new Dorothy P
tee shirt
and wedge heels

it feels hard to be stood up
by your first crush
in your rush
to be grown up
when
he's eleven
and you're ten

Hobbies, a History

my origami class
folded
jewellery making
lost its shine
the potholing group
went under
history forum
ran out of time
birdwatching
made me twitchy
my book club
lost the plot
I couldn't get hooked
on crochet
woodwork succumbed

to dry rot
my skydiving lessons
went bump
yoga class
ran out of zen
I thought that calligraphy
might be for me
but I just couldn't master the pen
embroidery
had me in stitches
trainspotting
ran out of steam
I'm not cut out for this hobbying lark
…but wait
there's an ice hockey team…

Letter to My Thirteen-Year-Old Self

Do not wish for a bigger chest
it may come true and then
at best weigh you down
literally
and there will be
a not inconsiderable cost in
downsizing

do not, ever, think you are fat
and that your hair should be straight
or wait to moisturise
or bemoan the size
of your thighs
for you are perfect just as you are

don't follow the crowd
not allowed to voice a different opinion
be no one's minion
find out what you're about
and shout your uniqueness
from the rooftops at every opportunity

talk to your grandparents
while they're still around
you may have found them dull
but they have lessons full
of wisdom and experience
that you'll wish
you'd learnt when it's too late

say yes to opportunity
some of it may be
bad or mad or dangerous
or onerous
but at least you gave it a go
so that when you're as old as me
you'll see the colourful
trail of your life and smile

Lumbar Lament

Wanted
New spine
(must have associated muscles, discs, etc. attached)
Any reasonable price considered
Willing to travel

For sale
Vintage spine
(has all associated muscles, discs, etc.)
Suitable for restoration project
Or may be useful for parts

Reasons for sale
1970s processed-food diet
Pregnancy (twice)
Stiletto heels

Dr Scholl's sandals (the cheap, rip-off ones)
Lifting small children without bending knees
Lifting large children without bending knees
Gardening (but not a lot)
Lack of yoga (until it's getting too late)
Gaining weight
Losing weight
Gaining weight
Losing weight (repeat last two lines ad infinitum)
Climbing in and out of cars
Lack of good sleep
Excessive overindulgence (specifics deleted by censors)

Asking price
Free to good home
Willing to deliver (but buyer must lift out of car boot)

Massage in a Northern Town

I'm lying on a massage table
in a gritty northern town
while a girl whose name tag reads *Harmony*
slaps my chakras up and down
there's music in the background
something soothing and slightly hippy
but somehow it can't disguise the fact
that the room is above a chippy
there may be salves with lavender
all the way from France
but it's hard to maintain focus when
you've nothing on but your pants
'your energy levels aren't great,' she says,
'I can feel that they are dipping,'
but I can't concentrate on anything
all I'm sensing is hot beef dripping

'let me cleanse your aura for you
and open up your pores,'
but hovering above the perfumed oil
an aroma of curry sauce
'just relax and meditate
let me put you at your ease,'
when all that I can think of
is fish and mushy peas
perhaps it's the same at Champneys
the smells of lobster bisque
at least this is only twenty quid
not three hundred pounds (at least)
'there, doesn't that feel better,'
she croons when an hour passes, or three
'that's great, many thanks,' I mumble
as I shoot down the stairs for my tea.

The Mind Reader

why can't you read my mind?
she thinks
ironically
and see that I'd really like a cup of tea
made for me
by you
you, who would make me one if I asked
but that's not the point

why can't you pre-empt my needs?
she pleads
inside her head
instead, she makes her own tea
and sulks

what's wrong?
he asks
was there some task that you
wanted me to do?
it's nothing
she shrugs
putting the mugs away
and seething

why can't he fathom her unsaid meaning?

it's so hard to find
she thinks
a mind
reader
these days

The Should Shouters

'You should do dry January,' they said
who are these powerful shoulds?
so I thought I would
but bloody hell
January is a long month
with its dreary clouds
I allowed myself just a small one

February is shorter
it oughter (sorry)
be easy peasy lemon squeezy
but some idiot put Valentine's day in there and,
to be fair, who wants a sober snog these days

March may be a better bet
and yet with spirits low
and talk of snow, hey-ho

April looks a bit more likely
me thinks – hints of spring when the thing is
we want to celebrate with fizz

And May may, if I may say,
be bring-out-the-barbecue time
scrape off the rust and dust down the sausage-
 spattered grill
that will obviously call for a margarita to greet
the summer

And June? June is sometimes a bummer it's true,
hard to get through without a tipple to toast the
 ripples of rain
flooding the bottom of the garden
again
perhaps those who shout should
should just
be a bit more reasonable

The Very Hungry Dieter

The very hungry dieter lay in her bed
a little longer than usual
to skip breakfast
which is *good* they said
at ten o'clock she ate
two blueberries,
at eleven o'clock she ate
a Ryvita, dry,
which is hard to do – try it
at twelve o'clock she ate
two tomatoes and a slice of cheese
no carbs, please
at two o'clock
having starved herself for an hour
showing great willpower
she ate
half an apple
at three o'clock she ate
the other half
at four o'clock she ate
a spoonful of peanut butter
from the jar – for the protein
and, which was quite bizarre,

still felt hungry
at six o'clock she ate
five chocolate digestives, two packets of crisps,
one Tesco Finest carbonara
two (small) pots of Ambrosia creamed rice,
two squares of chocolate
two squares of chocolate
two squares of chocolate
one slice of toast with butter and jam
three slices of air-dried ham
two gherkins
half a bag of oven chips
a pack of Doritos with various dips
and one bottle of wine
and, after a time,
the very hungry dieter
felt a little sick

the very hungry dieter lay in her bed
a little longer than usual
to skip breakfast
which is *good*

Poems About Motherhood

I recently had the absolute joy of becoming a grandma for the first time and it brought back vivid memories of the joy, anxiety and sheer exhaustion of motherhood. Many glossy television adverts would have us believe that new mums (and dads) wander round with beatific smiles in pristine, colour-coordinated homes, cooing over babies who appear never to scream or have shit up their backs whilst you cry into the small hours with sick on your dressing gown.

Wake up, advertisers: your products would be far more attractive if you showed both sides of the story!

These poems are dedicated to my two beautiful children and to the warrior mums and dads who manage to survive, suffused with more love than they knew existed.

Maternal Roller Coaster

That small bundle in your arms
that flesh against flesh
the mewling helplessness
is the most powerful creature on earth
for their joy is yours
their pain your pain
their woes are yours to soothe
until,
their hugs are virtual, skyped glimpses
power no less diminished by time or seas
cherish them
and the richness of the maternal roller coaster.

Little Brother

we bought you a doll
so that
when you came to visit your new brother
in the hospital
you'd associate something good
with his birth
when in fact
after looking at the doll
with utter
disdain
you proclaimed,
'Where's the baby?'
And you held him more gently
than we'd guessed you would
and asked,
genuinely interested,
if we could
'open its feets'!

You poked, prodded,
bossed, cajoled,
scolded and loved
that baby brother
all the way to manhood.
But don't, anymore,
ask to see his feet.

Do You Remember?

Do you remember
when we bathed you
in the sink
I don't think so
or the 3am lullabies
with tired eyes
and aching arms
your charms the only thing keeping
us awake
waiting to take
our chance at rest
knowing at best we'd get ten minutes
straight?
The late-night milky smiles
all the while capturing
a little more of our hearts
the part of us that
had been unutterably changed

for the better
or the wondering sighs
at the size of your tiny
fingers
and toes
and rows of
beautifully perfect
eyelashes
the dashes
to late-night chemists
for nappy rash
cream
it seems
you won't remember
when we were your all
and you were ours

Lines to a Daughter...

when we brought you home
swaddled and new
we said
when will she smile?
and you did
and we savoured those smiles
and put them in a book
with the date

swaddled and new
we said
when will she crawl?
and you did
and we chased those crawls
wreathed in giggles and mischief
and we put them in a book
with the date

we said
when will she walk?
and you did
and you were off
unsteady and stumbling
and we stood ten feet tall to have

brought into the world a walking, giggling
little girl
and we put it in the book
with the date

when will she walk?
what will she do?
and you grew and discovered
life for yourself and
little by little
you needed us less
we didn't put that in the book

what will she do?
and now your heart is full of the future
and all of our dreams for you have come true
and you will write a book of your own
filled with more love than you can know
when we brought you home

Mother and Child

I see him nuzzled against her breast
and suddenly all other lives
have become this one
the focus
on her son
so intense that
all of the world is blurred
each word
weighted by this new life
this pull of motherhood
that eclipses the strongest love
she's known
as this tiny, growing form
is more
encompassing
than all that has gone before

as nature weaves its web
of a bond that is fierce
and strong
and will last
long after he doesn't
need her anymore
but here
in this moment
there is only mother and child
and a knowing that every smile
and gurgle
and cry
and sigh
and gaze
and haze of milk-sated sleepiness
deepens

Nobody Told Me

As soon as I knew,
as soon as that blue line
appeared in the little window
I prepared and dared to dream
I read all the books
and took all the classes
to get ready for you
this new love of my life.
And you grew
and I knew
that this would be the
biggest adventure
nothing but joy – girl or boy
and imagined you there
in my arms
protected and content
safe from harm
but no manual I'd read
ever said how hard
those first few days would be
how I couldn't see
beyond the next feed

and the need to sleep, just sleep
would be overwhelming.
No one warned me of the anxiety
that saw me watching you breathe
and sigh and cry
not knowing whether what I
was doing was right
those middle-of-the-night pacings
facing long hours of wakefulness
and long days of well-meaning
visits and gifts
when all I wanted to do
was give you back – for a while –
rather than smile and pretend I was fine
I couldn't see a path through
but then you slept for one
whole
blissful hour
and I had a shower
and began to feel
human again
and completely in love.

Waiting to be a Granny

Today I can't settle,
my mind is fizzing and flitting
like a fizzy flitty thing
as I wait for you
and wonder whose bet'll
win the baby weight sweep.
My sleep
in this heat of expectation
this anticipation
of elation
is sporadic at best.
No rest
for the wicked, they say
well I guess that today
I'll just prop open my eyes

and stay awake
waiting for news
cooking stews
and cottage pies
the size
of a cottage.
Filling the freezer
to ease
the sleepless nights
that are sure to come
at some stage.
It's hard being the waiter
but far greater
your labour.
Literally.

One Day

One day he'll be too big for this
he'll shrug off your attempts
to hug him
in a slouch of attitude and acne
of slammed doors and blushes
of rushing off before you can
remind him that he is loved
and to be safe out there
beware of strangers
of dangers
that he's longing to face
at a pace that
leaves you breathless
and remembering when everything
he was
was held in your arms
and you could keep him safe
just know that those expressions of love
that now tug at your heartstrings
are the foundations of his
confidence
to face life's adventures.

Poems About Life, Love and Grief

I hope there will be poems in here that will speak of your own experience. So many of life's events are common to us all. I think that the more we share these, the more we can empathise with each other. After all, we've all been there.

I Am Made From

I am made from marbles in the cul-de-sac gutter
from *Two-Way Family Favourites* and powdered soup
Janet and John
Valerie Singleton and Peter Purves' *Blue Peter*
baking bread that stings the eyes
twin tubs and Monday polished shoes
from the quiet of a Thursday evening library,
children's section
I am made from a sturdy ring-dial telephone
'Pyramid 3581, who's speaking please?'
from sandwiches in sweaty plastic Tupperware
in the leg-burning back seat of a blue Ford Anglia
from the anxiety of fielding in rounders
the gasps and pants at the back of the cross-country run
the burning cheeks of the girl
whose father farted, loudly, at public occasions
from a 'should wear pink and play with dolls' time
the dared to steal sweets from the shop time
a stay-at-home mum
tea on the table and clean sheets time
from the smell of cheese-and-onion omelettes
and the theme music from *Match of the Day*
lying awake and listening for my dad's key in the door
I am made from a vanished world.

My Mum...

My mum borrowed a dress
to go to a dinner dance
with my dinner-suited dad
it was pink chiffon
with sequined collar and cuffs
and she wafted around
in a cloud of Coty L'Aimant
and I thought
she was the most beautiful
thing in the world.

My mum drank a glass of water
and let me lie
with my head on her tummy
to listen to the gurgling of
her insides
we laughed 'til we cried
and she drank some more.

My mum got the giggles
watching a sketch on the
two Ronnies
on a Saturday night
and laughed so hard
that she wet herself – and I was thrilled.

My mum cried when she
realised that she wouldn't
survive
to see her grandchildren.
She didn't.

My daughter watched
me get ready for a party
in my sparkly dress
and her eyes shone.

I drank a glass of water
and we laughed as she
rested her head on my
tummy and listened to the gurgles.

I laughed so hard at Victoria Wood
that I wet myself,
just a little – and she was thrilled

Still...

I love you even though
you think salads are the work of the devil
make a chilli that's too hot for me to eat
and have no time for the French
you can make your glass of wine last longer than mine
but never put your pots in the dishwasher
you do an impressive front crawl – and I can't
you don't like Michael Bublé
and because
you booked tickets and came with me to see Michael Bublé
you can do maths
you have great shoulders
and can fix a car, or a washing machine, or a fridge
you give a good head massage
you ring, in the newspaper, TV programmes that you think I'd like to watch
and buy me the expensive peanut butter
and a dozen new books every Christmas
you love our children fiercely
and did a job that you sometimes hated so that I could study
you like my Yorkshire puddings and say they're better than Aunt Bessie's
you understand now what family means, even when for so long you did not.

March Morning, 1954

my dad went rowing
on the morning of his wedding
with his best man Bob
on the lake
and they didn't know the first thing
about rowing
or getting married

it was early
neither had slept
narrow 1950s hotel beds
their backs ached
they dipped quiet oars
into misted waters
a fish jumped
at least it could have been a fish
fish came from the fishmongers where they were from
and it was becoming clear
that wedding shoes and new, stiff suits
from Donne's
were not well suited to March dawn paddles
in the North of England
they stood at the altar,
   slightly damp

the lake
that we would visit as children
and adults and husbands and wives
mothers and fathers
grandmothers and grandfathers
sometimes rowing
sometimes watching the gentle waves
and the soft breeze
this place that brought together my parents
not so many jumping fish these days
and no Father
no Mother
and no Uncle Bob

The Shared Peach

I wonder if you remember?
We walked along warm
unfamiliar
pavements
and you bought a peach
from a walnut-faced lady
with olive eyes
and she placed it
tenderly as a fuzzy newborn
into a paper bag

we sat on the stone steps in the sun
and shared the peach
its sweet flesh soft between juiced lips
tasting of love

and we gazed up at the magnificent cathedral
that we did not visit

I still have the peach stone
in a box
I wonder if you knew that?

Today

Today
I think you knew me
for a second
your eyes saw something in mine
that was familiar.

I think you knew me
and I didn't want you
to know me
for if you do
what else do you know?

And I didn't want you to
know that you need to be
lifted
and fed
and cleaned
and moved to prevent sores.

I hope you don't know
that you cannot find the words
that your shouts of frustration
cannot, anymore,
be understood.

That you cannot find the words
to say you love me.
That you remember pushing me on the swing
just a bit too high,
or laughing together at the
dinner table.

To say you love me.
And I must hold
those memories for both of us
and pray the unnatural prayer
that you'll soon be gone.
Today, I think you knew me.

The Shed

sweet peas,
a small bunch tied with string
at the allotment
picked and arranged in the shed,
a self-build of discarded wood and window frames,
WD40, cans of lubricating oil,
slug pellets, onion setts, mildew,
packets of seed, folded,
clipped with wooden clothes pegs,
boxes of mismatched screws – you never knew,
Great-Grandad's spade, like Trigger's broom –
on its seventh handle,
bamboo sticks, twine,
garden gloves dried to the shape of his hands.

My Song

the lines on my body
sing my song
the long
pale stripes
and creases
tell my tale
and will not be denied
why hide
my history

sing my song
in the silver streaks
on my belly that shout
to the world
of the babies that curled
inside
one died
but two survived and thrived
and ring me now
when they get the time

my song, where
the folds around my eyes
bear witness
to times of laughter
and joyous tears
for the years have brought
me a heartful of both

my song where
the puckered tracks
across my butchered breasts
attest to a cancer that, this time,
did not win
to drugs and knives that let me
begin again

some songs have darker verses
and the livid-red bracelets
that circle my wrists?
I wish I could tell you they were an accident
but one day
many moons ago
when my skies were dark
they weren't

I'm Sorry

I'm sorry that you weren't planned
in my dreams your tiny hand curls around the coil
that was supposed to foil the eager sperm
but instead foiled you

in my dreams your tiny hand curls around the coil
as we prodded you with a needle
afraid you'd be less than perfect
and not prepared to countenance that fact

as we prodded you with a needle
and you felt unwanted
the idea of you, in those early days, too much to comprehend
how could I know that to lose you
would leave you with me for ever

and you felt unwanted
battered and bruised
abused
you chose to leave
to heave yourself from my body without a cry

battered and bruised
I wonder today what your nineteen-year-old life would have been
would you have your brother's smile
your sister's hands
your father's eyes
or my guilt for not wanting you enough for you to survive?
I'm sorry that you weren't planned

Weight of Grief

It's like
she said
waiting for a thunderstorm
to strike
to clear the air
that's lying hot and humid
making me aware
of every breath
and the heaviness of every limb
it feels as if death
didn't just happen to him
but to me
every thought an effort
I can't see
my next hour
let alone my next twenty-four
haven't the power
to string
sentences
together
in any
kind of
meaningful way
leaning into

this grief
and not knowing
the relief of
how
or when
I will be able to lean away
take each day
they say
one at a time
but how can I find
a way to take
the next breath?

Anstey's Cove, 1933

What colour was that dress?
I think my hat was palest pink
'What do you think?'
I said, 'I'm not sure'
'Wear it,' you said,
'you look beautiful

I remember your shoes were new
and raised blisters on your toes
as we strode along the beach
out of the reach of disapproving eyes

a moment of unadulterated joy
remember the boy who took the photo?
He was walking by
and we asked him to take the shot
he didn't care a jot
for our forbidden embrace

how long did we live as just friends
meeting at the end of the day
longing to be together
but doubtful whether
we were brave enough?

I look around today
at those who are out and proud and gay
and I wonder what might have been
I would love to have seen
you grow old
in my arms

Dark Days...

When grey clouds seep into my mind
I find
the colours of spring,
once so bright,
have faded now to black and white.
The clouds seep in and then there comes
a disturbed equilibrium
though I know there's joy
I can see and hear
somehow it's seen through
mists of anxiety and fear
my logical brain knows this will pass,
the world will come back through a brighter glass,
but until the clouds roll away,
I will paste on a smile
and find a way to join in the jokes
keep repeating 'I'm fine'
and telling myself
with time
the colours will shine again,
until then
take care, be kind
for we don't know what troubles
the next person's mind.

Have My Seat

have my seat, he says
and she glances down at this boy-man
with his dark lashes and red coat
beginning to unravel his legs and stand
in the misty-windowed rush-hour bus
the fuss and forbearance of
stranger pushed tight against stranger
street lights struggling to cast their light
through the drizzle of a winter night
please, sit here, he says again
and she wonders, for an instant, who he is talking to
the pain in her hip, her liver-spotted hand gripping
   the seat rail
reminding her that she has slipped
into old age without really noticing
and she realises,
with what shouldn't be a shock but is,
that he's speaking to her

Don't Assume You Know

Don't think that these feet
in their sensible shoes
haven't danced
in red high heels
cartwheeled on the grass
in the last of the night's chill

or that this grey hair
styled with care
wasn't once bright red
then blue
then, once, I remember,
green
hasn't seen perms come and go
didn't sport, famously, a bow
in a school photograph

don't believe that this whispered voice
warbling its way through a remembered song
was always so soft
it was held aloft, loud and proud
and ringing the rafters of many a hall
barrow-boy calls to the lads in the street
the witty repost not lost, still there

and this tired old heart
with its faltering beat
has felt the heat of more passion
than you're likely to know
slow burns and fast falls
broken more times than I can recall

you may think you know me
you don't know me at all

Facts

I know you don't like fiction
find poetry too obscure
so I'm hoping you'll read my factual rhyme called
I don't love you anymore.

Swallows are migratory
they fly, annually, thousands of miles
for the last ten years of our marriage
I've been mostly faking the smiles.

A day on the planet Pluto
lasts approximately ninety-three hours
I've been crying, usually twice a day,
when you've thought I've been taking showers.

The African bullfrog can spit
further than all other toads
I've tried to rekindle my love for you
but I think it's the end of the road.

A rattlesnake, when startled,
can leap several metres high
I know that you know I've been sad lately
but not once have you asked me why.

The annual Tiddlywinks World Cup
is held in Pakistan
I don't think you'll believe me when I say that I'm
    leaving,
but it's true,
actually, I am.

And just to add insult to injury
(and I think this will really gall you)
some of the 'facts' listed above
may, or may not, be true*

*apart from the fact that I don't love you anymore.
    That's true.

I'm Fine

I am fine
a dangerous line
that we teach our children
from the first knee that's bruised
we choose
to hold that mask,
tasked with ensuring
the ease of others
we mothers, fathers,
sisters, brothers
'you're fine'
so that
even when
it's not a knee that is hurt
but a
heart
we tell the world
that we're fine

maybe if we dropped the mask
and when asked
responded in truth that we're
sad
or angry
or adrift
maybe others would lift their eyes
and recognise that
we all have times when we need
to chime
I'm not fine… but I will be

Last Night...

Last night I dreamt of you
again
you were in my grandma's kitchen
where you'd never been
amongst a sea of people
who I did not know
and I had to say excuse me
a hundred times
past chattering strangers
to reach the place
where you were rolling the floured pastry
for a blackberry pie
and you turned your back on me.

Last night I dreamt of you
again
and we walked along the shore
of a travel-brochure beach
and strayed into the waves
out of our depth
and the seaweed wrapped around my feet
and I couldn't reach you.

Last night I dreamt of you
again
or I thought I did
for I heard your voice
as I walked along the street
every sound was you
but what was new
as I increased my pace
heart pounding
was that
I couldn't
remember
your
face

Most of the Time

most of the time
you aren't on my mind
I find that the gaps between
my thoughts of you
grow longer and those
moments when I do
think of you
are a little less sad
still bad
sometimes
but more about a
memory – often a happy one
a funny one
a mad one
and less about the
anguish of losing you
as they say so rightly
bit by bit

I think that you would
like to know
that we show
your great-grandson
photos of you
and say that was your
great-grandad
who had the same name as you
and who was mostly great
but was sometimes an
awkward bugger

I think you'd like that

Miscellaneous Poems

All the bits that didn't quite fit into the other categories!

Sometimes ideas for poems occur to me in the oddest of places: the bath, in traffic jams on the M6 (why is it always the M6?), watching a supposedly absorbing and brilliant film. I think the seeds of these come from things that have happened to me or from stories I've heard, even news items that I'm powerless to respond to other than to write down how I feel about them.

Enough

I do not wake in sheets of silk
or smooth Egyptian cotton, ironed and neat
but my sleep is just as sweet
in Tesco Easycare
and how dare I grumble
when others dream of a clean bed.

I do not breakfast on kedgeree
or exotic fruit from far-off lands
my bread is somewhat bland
and made in a factory
but nothing gives me the right
to complain
when plain is a luxury for some.

This morning I will not dress in Chanel
or Louis Vuitton
I will not put on jewels and Jimmy Choos
my shoes will be sturdy
and keep out the rain
but not for me the pain
of bare feet or thin soles in the snow.

Today I will not walk amongst majestic hills
taking my fill of verdant forests and leafy glades
I may
if the weather holds
venture to my local park
and watch the children feed the ducks
and think how lucky I am
to have somewhere to go
and someone to walk with.

It seems we live in times of greed
constantly told what we *need*
that more is more
the latest, fastest, newest, most luxurious
must be had
is it so bad
to be grateful for enough
when enough would be riches for some?

Autumn Lines

this morning
as the oh, so small
and shiny little ones
trooped off for their first
day of school
the air felt cool
and the sun
though warm
had lost its bite
the light
a golden haze
ushering shorter days
and jewelled trees
bedecked and
easing off their summer green
the first sheens of frost
on early lawns
and dawn's back to work
and routine
it seems the long hot
summer
has had its day
and makes way for something

more British
than beaches and parched grass
the familiarity of drizzle
and the mizzle of an early fog
the dream of another log
on the fire
as the pyre of summer's bounty
feeds the bonfires of
an autumn afternoon

Canal Cormorant (Phalacrocorax Carbo)

Deserted Tuesday morning towpath
up above the clamour of the retail park
pausing to take a breath
my eye catches his as he surfaces
black and sleek
raising his beak
and shaking jewelled droplets from his feathers
in a
just-look-at-me-aren't-I-gorgeous
kind of way
and I smile
reaching for my phone to take a photo
of his glorious summer sheen
a scene to be captured
enraptured
I fumble
and he's gone
diving in an instant
a bright needle into black silk

effortless

I wait and watch
and in a time-stretched moment

he surfaces
winking and arching at his own prowess
told you I was the best
he winks
a good ten metres from his entry point
repeating his performance for his solitary audience
until
chest out
he glides away

and I walk on

Drizzle

today the air has lost its weight
a drizzle that's much more British
falls from slate-grey skies
and the gardens sigh
with relief

so I should dust
I guess
clear up the mess in the spare room
get out the broom
pay the overdue bills
wipe down windowsills

but it seems there will always be
to me
more interesting ways to spend my time
I find
than lining up my soup tins
or cleaning the sink's overflow

I could go
and start a fresh new book
from the pile by my bed
or, instead,
just watch the sky
and wonder why
I can't quite get that colour of blue
on my palette
or let the rain
just be
with me
in it
savouring its coolness

Hidden Agenda

the agenda of a *woman's magazine*
it seems to me
has told me over the years
subliminally
that I mustn't be…
that I'm…

too clever by half
too dumb to take part
too clumsy to run
too fussy for fun
too tall to compete
too short
two left feet

too dumb to take part
too fat for my heart
too curved to fit in
too spotty a skin
too dull a complexion
no right connections

too fat for my heart
wrong hair for a start
wrong style of dress
nails are a mess
wrong occasion, wrong shoe
wrong shade of blue

wrong hair for a start
wrong views, set apart,
too right
too left
wrong weave
wrong weft

do not believe
you are any of these things
do and be only what brings
you joy
for you are a perfect you
heaven sent and were not meant
to be what the magazine
editors decreed
that you need to be
you are, simply, you

If I'm Honest...

if I'm honest, I've been avoiding the news
the views of horrors and war
that, unbelievably, have paused
ordinary lives
the mother clutching a toddler who should be
playing with his friends at nursery
now sits quietly in a bunker while
around him neighbours hunker
waiting for the next shells to rain down
as all around, shop workers, hairdressers,
architects, baristas, managers, taxi drivers,
put their lives on hold
listening as destruction unfolds
in their
quiet residential streets

if I'm honest, I've been avoiding the news,
small, everyday worlds upended in a
tidal wave of aggression, a power and land grab
mad
men
in marble halls
planning the fall
of communities and livelihoods

when will motherhood finally be free
from having to see fathers, husbands, brothers and sons
mown down by guns on the whim of a despot?
how quickly we forgot
the horrors that so recently
our grandfathers and grandmothers
hoped they'd never see again

if I'm honest, I've been avoiding the news,
for what can I do?
I can donate and say prayers
hope that soon, somewhere,
a flicker of sanity burns brighter than hate,
that peace will prevail
that it won't be too late and that
children who cower and cover their ears,
won't go on to suffer that hatred for years
will wear their yellow and blue with pride
in a country where nobody has to hide
and the small lives we all take for granted each day
may return

Turning a Blind Eye

Just look the other way, son,
pretend you did not see
don't worry about the safety regs
they won't trace you and me

just gloss over the fine print
we haven't got the time
you can't check all the details
if you want to make a dime

don't go for the costly option
the cheap stuff will work just as well
it looks the ticket
that's the trick
and the shareholder's pockets will swell

cut short the required inspections
we can save a huge amount
no one will notice
fewer will care
except our off-shore accounts

this time next week we'll be millionaires
we'll hit the big time
we'll succeed
the key to our murky fortunes?
it's simple, my lad, it's greed

Shocked by My Own Lethargy

the curtains stir with the promise
of a breeze that doesn't come
the cat pants and finds a small
patch of shade by the bookshelf
as dust motes settle
and I am shocked by my own lethargy

sleep evades the twisted sheets at night
and then pursues me during the day
draping its heavy weariness on my shoulders
and dripping its molten heat from my brow
and I am shocked by my own lethargy

I sigh as I sit,
picking up the half-finished book and reading
and rereading the same line
noticing that there are pots to be washed
and beds to be made
and bills to pay
and plants to water
and still, I am shocked by my own lethargy

perhaps I can raise the energy
to go to the pub
for a cold clear pint
but then again
my shoes are upstairs…

Autumn's Approach

the hint of a morning chill
the edge of a leaf readying itself
for an autumn flourish
a fallen, smooth-skinned conker
irresistible and cool
to the touch
much is made of summer
with its enforced fun and
barbecue vibe
but
truth be told
I love to be enfolded
by autumn
when a bright day
dazzles
and the crisp leaves rustle
as I walk
under an azure sky

Grandma

The cupboard in the corner of the room
houses treats
forbidden at home:
jam, white sliced bread
tinned, plump mandarins
the 'grandma tea' cupboard
that she reaches into
Penguin biscuits, a whole pack,
Fox's glacier mints
in the kitchen a meat safe
with netted door
who knew what for
we were wary of the need
to keep meat safe –
from what?
Enormous bath in tiny bathroom
yellowing enamel
and a giant-sized tin of floral air
freshener that stung the eyes
drop-leaf table that doubled as a cave
on rainy days
but was awkward if you had to sit next to the leg
sparking static in a nylon overall
sleeves rolled
Grandma ready at a moment's notice to conjure pastry
for foraged blackberries

Someone Else's Tune

if you follow the path of pleasing others
fathers, mothers,
sisters, brothers,
the path of pleasing
seizing
every chance
to be praised
and raised to be polite
not fight the rules
schooled
in doing the right thing
singing someone else's tune
then soon
before you know it
your path won't be your own
but mown by fulfilling
the needs of the rest
at best
pleasant
and predictable
but not discernibly
your own
listen to advice
be, generally, nice

but make that path your own
grown
from your own thoughts
and ideas
without fear
of striking out
of taking
a path of your own making
even if it is
the road less travelled.

About the Author

Sally Lang is a retired teacher whose work aims to capture the magical in the mundane. Poems that resonate with the lived experience of most of us, from the ups and downs of motherhood to the effects of an unexpected heatwave, there's something in here for everyone. Which poem will you identify with the most?